Jesus and Me
I Walk Alone

MAUDE MASSEY

Copyright © 2011 Maude Massey

All rights reserved.

ISBN:1466288485

DEDICATION

I give Honor to the best Friend I ever had, my Savior to Whom I owe everything and to my five children.
also
To Sue Crocker for all her hard work.

CONTENTS

Foreword by Nona Freeman   ii

Preface by Deb Massey Dueitt   iii

1. My early years   Pg #1
2. Our daily life   Pg #9
3. My convictions   Pg #21
4. Meet Delbert Massey   Pg #27
5. Our family   Pg #35
6. Delbert's health   Pg #41
7. My premonition   Pg #53
8. Life after Delbert   Pg #59
9. Making a living Jesus and me   Pg #65

10	Growing family	Pg #71
11	Health and miracles	Pg#79
12	Grandchildren miracles	Pg#91
13	Shoulder surgery	Pg#99
14	Burden for Bobbie Jo	Pg#105
15	Jesus stays the storm	Pg#109
16	Meeting Jennifer	Pg#115
17	Test of faith	Pg#121
18	I don't regret a mile	Pg#139
19	Poem written by my sister	Pg#143
20	Gems from Paulette	Pg#147
21	Poem "The Widow"	Pg#153

ACKNOWLEDGMENTS

Compiled and Edited by:
Sue Massey Crocker

All pictures and content in this book property of:
Sue Massey Crocker
and
Deb Massey Dueitt

All rights reserved. No part of this book, including cover design and photographs, may be reproduced or transmitted in any form or by any means, electronic or mechanical, including photocopying, recording or by information storage and retrieval system- without written permission from the author, except by a receiver who may quote brief passages in a review to be printed in a magazine or newspaper.

MAUDE MASSEY

FORWARD
BY NONA FREEMAN

As you take the journey with me through these anointed pages; you will laugh and you will cry tears of joy as you marvel at how anyone with only an eighth grade education survived. Widowed at twenty-six years of age and left with five children Maude Massey is the first to tell you, 'I did not make it alone, it was Jesus and Me!' You will believe in miracles after reading her story. Nona Freeman 2008

PREFACE

I have had the honor of having mother live with us in her senior years. One thing I vividly remember growing up; is nobody crossed mother's children. She is 84 years old now and if you want to see an ole granny turn into a she bear; bother one of us. It has been my desire for mother to feel as safe and happy in her older years as she made us feel growing up. I thought I was helping her but it is she that really helps me.

I have walked through the house and heard mother in her bedroom talking to our Lord. I have drunk coffee with her every morning and listen as she would tell of the many times Jesus saw us through. There is no way a book could hold all of her wonders of Jesus and how He kept this widow woman and her five children. Don't ask me how but mother managed to make everyone of us feel like her favorite. To tell the truth every one of us holds a special place in her heart. We didn't have a daddy growing up but we had a wonderful living and how she was successful; it was Jesus.

I always felt safe and felt mother could do anything. I still find myself going to her and she helps me know what to do. I don't know how much longer we will have with mother; I do hope we all get to go in the rapture. But if that is not in God's plan for us; I will try to do as she has taught us though I can't picture life without her.

She has been this family's rock. She is our queen, a shoulder to lean on and a soft hand to hold. The word of God says her children's price is far above rubies and her children call her blessed. In a world where people are turning their back on God, He looks down on a little widow woman and her five children. His word has proven true; don't mess with a widow and her children. Some have tried, but where are they now?

I look back now that I am older and didn't have a male figure in my life for protection. We had Papa Moore but not a daddy. I can truly say I didn't worry or fear anyone, because I knew we had a 'she bear' and no one could get by bothering with her babies. My sister Connie says it best, 'Although we are adults, sometimes in life no matter how old I get; no one else will do; I just have to talk to mother.' This is so true and even now as adults with children and grandchildren of our own; you still better not cross her children.

In May of 2009 tests revealed our mother had to have surgery to remove a golf ball sized tumor in her colon. I looked around the waiting room at the people that was there to support her. There were six ministers she has mentored to setting there in support and honor of this mighty woman of Jesus. There was an employee in environmental services Sue wanted us to meet while mother was in the hospital. Seven doctors had told the family that there was no doubt, mother would have colon cancer. Well seven doctors were wrong. When the lady came to the door she heard mother talking about her good report; absolutely no cancer! As she enters the room instantly the Holy Ghost fell and the lady ended up in the bathroom shouting and speaking in that heavenly language.

If the Bible was still being written; mother would have a chapter where God remembered her. So if in reading her memoirs, if you are healed or moved to drawer closer to Jesus; be my guest. Her life has affected mine like that many times.

Her children call her blessed and her in-laws are her children too. They each have a special place in her heart. Probably Eddie will get the biggest reward because he keeps her turnips planted!

I have been so blessed over the years to witness mothers walk with Jesus in her older years. I have walked through the house and heard her in her room praying for one of us children.

The generations are here, grandchildren and great-grandchildren are now added to her children as her prayers goes on. Many ministers' names are called out in her time of prayer. When one of us has gone as far as we can; the Lord has given mother a word of wisdom just for us.

We love you mother. Thank you for all the times you told us about Jesus; for the tears and prayers.

Deb Massey Dueitt

MAUDE MASSEY

Maude Massey age 26
and
Debra Fay Massey Dueitt in 1953.

JESUS AND ME

1 MY EARLY YEARS

The earliest memories of my childhood were when we lived on the Grady Young place. I must have been three or four years old. I do remember the big pecan tree in the lane on one side and a big cedar tree on the other side. I remember Mama washing down the hill at a big spring. We used to chew gum from a sweet gum tree. Granny Evelyn and Grandpa Bud Davis lived in a log cabin with mud chinked in the cracks. I don't remember much more about those times because I was very young. Everyone was poor in those days but nobody knew they were poor. The first radio I ever remember was a neighbor who had one in his car and he would come to our house and let us listen to it. We thought that was something!

Uncle Charlie and Aunt Ed Davis; Grandpa Davis' son; Mama's step brother and sister lived just across the field from them and about a mile further is where Uncle Ash McLeod lived. Papa used to tell us all kinds of ghost stories about the Uncle Ash place. One of them was about a picture the family made after his wife died. She always wanted a family picture made and never made one until after her death. They finally made one after her funeral and when the picture was developed her head appeared in a tree. The only thing; there wasn't a tree there. I know that is true because when I was a teenager I saw the picture and sure enough the tree and her face are visible.

Mama's sisters, Aunt Maude and Aunt Susie, use to spend lots of time together. Aunt Maude had five children and Aunt Susie had four. One day Aunt Maude's son Rudolph and I was playing chase and he ran out a gate and slammed it shut. A nail stuck in my leg. I almost had blood poison from it. When I was real young Mama put a hot bowl of soup on the table and I pulled it off in my face. I still have the scar from the nail stick and the boiling soup.

My father William Albert Moore and Lela Stringer Moore on their wedding day December 25, 1912.

Papa was abused very badly as a child and for that reason he never whipped us and he could not tolerate for Mama to whip us either. Mama use to get after me and I would run to daddy and he would go round and round with me and take the licks for me. One day I was doing something and he had a board in his hands and he hit his leg and said, 'my goodness, I hit the baby with a board with a nail in it.' Boy everyone was mad at him. He was also a big teaser.

Papa worked on the rail road and had an accident and broke his leg.
With the money he got out of a settlement he bought the farm I was raised on. Papa was a very good farmer and he farmed a large farm with two old mules and a bad leg but he made some good crops. I don't ever remember him losing a crop.
At one time we owned another place but in those days you only had a handshake; daddy bought the place and back then you did not sign a contract; you just

shook hands and agreed. Later the man Papa bought it from said that he didn't pay for it and took it away; but Papa did pay him for it. Papa was very honest and had paid for the place all but $1,000.00; but the one that sold it to him beat him out of it. I was about three years old then but I remember the place well. Papa was very honest and taught all of us to be honest too.

The fondest memory of my childhood was sitting on the front porch in the evening time and listening to him tell tales; that was our television. We could hear the train whistle and he would tell us what every train whistle meant. My daddy never got over not working on the rail road. We would hear a whippoorwill call and he would say, 'it is time to plant cotton.' He made us a great living and Mama was a great helper. She canned everything she could get her hands on. They raised hogs and milked cows; and we had plenty of food even though it was depression years. They would hang meat and sausage in a smoke house and mine and Ina's duties was to keep the smoke going. That was good meat.

Ina and I played together all of our lives. We would nail a syrup can lid to a board and run up and down the lane. In the spring when the martin birds would build their nest we would make them run at us. They did not want us bothering with their birdies.

I remember when rainy weather would come we would put us a quilt at the end of the bed and tell stories. Papa use to have a horse named, John and he would paw any living thing he comes to. One day Ina and I were swinging down in the pasture and Papa turned John out. He got after us and we ran as fast as we could. Ina lost her hat and John pawed it all to pieces. He would have killed us if he had caught us. I always said if there is a hell for horses; John is there.

Child in front, Maude Moore Massey; Ina Moore Baygents in striped socks; Marie M. Williams and Charlie Moore 1930's.

My mother Lela Moore on left; Her mother Evelyn Davis in shawl ; Sisters, Susie Goff back and Maude Walters October 1958

2 OUR DAILY LIFE

We lived about a quarter of a mile from the church that I attended until I was grown. I never failed to get a whipping at church. I wish I could get as sleepy one time as I did when the preacher delivered his sermons. He preached one full hour by the clock and if you so much as nodded your head Mama would slap the fire out of you. I never could set still in my whole life and still can't to this day. A church member used to tell me if I would be still five minutes he would give me a dime. I never collected it. I was always bad in church and naturally sat with Ina.

Even if we were not doing one thing, Mama would look at us and shake her head.

Mama and Daddy in 1969

We always had lots of company; especially on Sunday after church. Mama was the world's greatest cook and in those days the grown folks ate first and the children last. If ever there was such a thing as child abuse that was it. They would eat all the best and then set there and talk while we all starved. Once in a while we would have potato salad and pineapple pudding and the grown folks got most of that. I swore if I ever got grown I would eat all the mayonnaise and pineapple I wanted.

Mama made most of our mayonnaise. She also made peanut butter, catsup, grits and other items that people take for granted now. A grocery order back then was like ten cents worth of rice, a quarters worth of salt meat; which was almost a whole side and maybe octagon soap was about all you could afford.

When we were children we didn't know much about electricity. Mama's half sister had electricity and what few times that we went to her house I thought that her refrigerator was something else! All of the ice that we knew about was from the ice truck that runs once or twice a week. It was in fifty or one hundred pound blocks. Mama would wrap it in an old quilt to keep it from melting. Later we got an ice box that you could put a block of ice in it and it would keep the rest of the box cool. Our hot water heater was what they called a reservoir. It was on the side of a wood stove; the stove that mama cooked on.

You could only use toilet soap which mama called sweet soaps to wash our faces. We all used the same wash cloth; which was a piece of a fertilizer sack but we only washed our face, hands and feet.

1929 Icebox

Mama made our panties out of fertilizer sacks because fertilizer came in beautiful sacks and it was beautiful fabric. One time we went to the river and Ina dove in at the sand bar. Her dress flew up and 'Big M' was stamped on the seat of her panties. I remember getting a good bath only when Mama washed clothes. She washed clothes down the hill at a big spring. When she got through she would put me and Ina in the last rinse water which was blue from washing denims or overalls. Mama use to make all our clothes and she would put a very small opening in the back. If our head would not go through it she would beat the fire out of us. I would say, 'Mama, I can't help it if my head is big!'

I know she had a hard time because there were seven of us. She stayed pregnant but of course she did not talk about that back then because it wasn't nice. About the only time we knew she was going to have another baby was when we had to spend the night at the neighbors. We knew then there would be another dead baby at our house. She had four stillborns after my birth. She had to work in the fields and didn't have the prenatal care like mothers do today. It grieved her to death when she lost her babies. Now we know that to be post partum depression but in those days nothing was known about it. She was the world's best mom.

They would bury four babies and one daughter in their life. Back then you dressed a stillborn baby yourself. Mama had stillborn twins, best I can figure this was circa 1933. Someone had dressed them when Mama saw them. She realized that she would never dress her babies; so she undressed each little baby and redressed them herself for their burial.

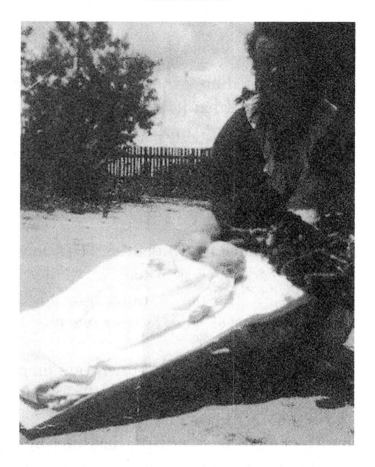

Paul and Talmadge Moore; twin sons stillborn to Mama and Papa circa 1933

One day Papa went to town and stayed almost all day. When he came home Mama asked him what he had been doing. He said that he had gone in every store in town. Mama told him, 'Turn around.' He had set down in battery acid and it had eaten the seat out of his overalls.

We did not have many luxuries. The only time we had tea was when we went to Aunt Susie's. I'll never forget how good it was. If we ever went to town we might get a cold drink.

Doctor Horn took me to town one time and bought me an Eskimo pie. That was the best something I had ever eaten.

It may sound like we had a bad life; but we had it lots better than many of our neighbors. Back in those days if a neighbor killed a hog or cow, they took all of the neighbors some and you had to walk to do that.

We would get together and rob bees for honey. If a neighbor had sickness, everyone would go set up with them. About all of the medication anyone had was Vicks salve and aspirin. Later on Upjohn came around for colds and such.

The first radio that came to our neighborhood was to the Smith family and everyone would gather down at their house and listen to the Grand Ole Opry on Saturday nights. We also had to walk to church nearly four miles. I remember pretending to be asleep so Mama or Charlie would carry me home. Mama always kept a very clean house. I can still see her beautiful white fertilizer sack sheets. Once for some reason I was at church alone, and my stomach was killing me. I got my uncle and aunt to walk home with me. I barely remember falling across the bed just knowing Mama would whip me for getting on her clean sheets. She didn't because I had pneumonia and was sick for many days.

Our bathroom was behind the smoke house. We did not have an indoor toilet for many years. My sister, Marie was the Christian of the crowd. She prayed every night. One night she was praying and Ina tickled her feet. She did not stop praying, but when she got through praying, she beat the fire out of Ina.

My childhood was a very happy one. Being the baby of the crowd of five sisters and one brother; I had it much easier than the rest. My idol was my daddy and in many ways; my worst influence. His blessing at the table was curse words. I remember how I wished Daddy would ask the blessing like my friend's dad. Later I learned he abused his children very badly.

I learned to use bad words exactly like my daddy; and to drink a toddy which is whiskey, water and sugar. Poor Mama would tell me that the booger man was going to get me. Daddy would just say no he won't; I'll stick my knife in him. I give my Mama credit for my walk with God today because she kept us in church. Daddy broke his leg on the rail road and it grew back crooked. He would tell people he got wet; lay down in the sun and warped it. Eventually he had to wear a high heel extension on that shoe. I would make him fix me one so I could be like him.

My dad Albert Moore circa 1970's

3 MY CONVICTIONS

All our lives Mama took us to church even though I always desired more. There was an empty place in my life even as a child that just didn't add up. I use to get behind the old walnut tree and pray. Even as a child God answered my prayers.

I always knew it was wrong to cut my hair, but I never told Mama how I felt. It wouldn't have done any good if I had because she was so full of pride. She couldn't stand for our hair not to be cut and curled. She would send me to Mobile to get a curl and I would go out under the pecan trees and look for a cloud to blow me away for cutting my hair. I was about eight years old then and had never heard of a Pentecostal church.

My childhood playmate and I use to pray the way we were raised to. She would pray a little and I would pray a little. We were raised strictly once saved; always saved but hard headed me could never be satisfied. Every time they had a revival; which we had once a year I would join again. I joined and was baptized three times and still knew I did not have anything.

I use to sleep with Mama and she never knew the turmoil that went through my young mind. I knew I was lost and would pray to myself way into the nights. One night I felt like I would die if I didn't get some relief. As I prayed a light just seemed to cover me up. I never felt such happiness in my life. If I had known how to seek God, I would have gotten the Holy Ghost that night.

Even though God dealt with me all my life, I was the meanest child Mama had. I cursed, smoked and drank some too and then would pray in to the night for God not to let me die in that shape. Ina was always my favorite sister and she was real quiet and good; so Mama thought. She wouldn't think of cursing and always tried to break me from the habit. She told me, 'Instead of cursing just grunt real big.' So one night before we had electric lights; we had company and Mama had put bed springs down in the floor to put a mattress on. Mama sent me in that room after something and it was very dark. I caught my foot on those springs and fell across them and it hurt so badly. Any how, I rose up and grunted real big like Ina told me to do. It did not help one bit so I cursed real big. What I did not know was that Ina was in there and heard me. She still laughs about it today.

When I was twelve years old, Mama began to keep boarders. Old trusty Ina fell in love with one of them and finally married him. I met one that I was sure I would love the rest of my life at about thirteen.

When I was about fourteen Ina and I moved to Mobile and got an apartment. Boy that was the wrong thing to do because at that age all I wanted was a good time; and that is just what I had. That was when Brookley Field was in full operation and there were plenty of soldiers there. It was the mercy of God that I ever lived to see home again. I would party most of the night and pray the rest. One time a soldier I had never seen before was on a motorcycle and stopped me on the street. He asked me if I wanted a ride and I crawled on. We rode a way off and turned around and came back. Nothing else happened. If God hadn't kept His hand on me I would never have made it through all that.

When Ina and I moved to Mobile we went wild as rabbits. I remember being in a bar with the gang and stayed until the buses quit running. I didn't have money for a taxi. Can you picture a fourteen year old; piney wood rutter standing on a deserted street in downtown Mobile? Nobody knew where I was and nobody cared except God; it had to be God that took care of me. I went to many bars with Brookley Field soldiers but God kept his hand on me all the way. One night Ina and I went to the movies and I had a horrible toothache. I was always condemned about going to the movies but went anyhow. I closed my eyes and said, 'God, if you would, you could stop this toothache.' Just like a flash it quit hurting. I truly was born to serve the Lord.

Delbert Massey Circa 1940's

4 MEET DELBERT MASSEY

In 1943, I met Delbert Massey, while dating his friend. When I met Delbert, my heart I lost! If I had known my destiny that day, I would have run like a scalded dog! I knew that day that I loved him but he was in the army and had to leave in three days. I was sure that I would never see him again, but what I didn't know was that cupid was working on both sides. He went in the house and told someone, 'See that girl out there in that car? Well I love her and I am going to marry her.

His brother was also in the service because the country was in World War II, and had to be back at Camp Shelby that night so Delbert made it his business to keep him out until it was too late to take me home before taking his brother to Shelby then take me home. When he did finally take me home we sure got acquainted that night. We dated three times and became engaged and had to court through the mail. His friend that I was dating wouldn't give up and he broke us up several times. He would tell Delbert I was running around on him, which I was but I always managed to convince him I wasn't.

We married seven months later and I never ran around on him again. After we married we would listen to the radio. The song, 'I Walk Alone,' would play all the time. It would almost kill me to hear it after he left. I never dreamed that would be my signature song and my destiny.

I Walk Alone

I walk alone where once we wandered;
It seems so strange that you are gone,
'Till you return, I'll stay the same dear;
I'll still be true and walk alone.
The flames of love are brightly burning,
You know that I'm your very own,
'Till you return, I'll stay the same dear;
I'll still be true and walk alone.

After we married on January 28, 1944, Delbert went back to camp at Indiantown Gap, Pennsylvania. He sent for me and I was so happy. I was ready to go and got a telegram that read, 'Don't come, a letter will follow to explain.' They only gave a few minutes to write a very brief one.

They were shipping him to France. I stood in the rain and read it. I was so hurt I didn't care about the rain; I just loved him so much. I was only sixteen at the time. We were married three days and separated twenty two long months. I was so lonely. He was in France, Germany and Japan during many invasions. I prayed for him daily; especially for God not to let him be in a battle. He told me later he was close enough to hear battles; but never got in one. June 6, 1944, was the invasion called, D-Day when over three thousand Americans was killed. God was with us even then and I wasn't even living for Jesus.

After he came home from the war I would wake up sometimes and he would be leaning on his elbow just staring down at me. I would wake up and ask him, 'What are you doing?' He would say, 'You are so pretty, I just love to watch you sleep.' I knew he loved me so much. I never told any of the children; but their dad was quite a Romeo.

There was never a day that he didn't tell me repeatedly, how much he loves me. If he was working in the garden he would take me a chair out there to set in. He said when he was away from me so long, in the service that he promised himself; if he ever got home that he would never spend another night away from me; and he meant it. He would go on fishing trips with men and they would say, 'Delbert won't stay all night,' and he wouldn't. From the first time that he laid eyes on me, until he took his last breath, I was the love of his life. When he came home we moved into a place of our own. Dorothy and I was moving furniture around and I pulled on a chest of drawers and tore my kidney loose. I passed a lot of blood and finally had to go to a specialist. He told Mama there was nothing he could do but operate. He said I would have to lie on my stomach seventeen days. I did not have the surgery and I had this trouble until after Paulette was born. I could not do my house work or anything.

One day I was lying on my bed with Paulette and I could not even tend to her. I just closed my eyes and said, 'God, if you will help me to be able to tend to my baby, I'll tell everyone.' God worked a miracle that day and I have been healed ever since; but I did not tell of my healing until after I got the Holy Ghost; God looked ahead.

Paulette who was born October 28, 1946, was a sickly child and we almost lost her when she was about three years old. Delbert did not believe in taking medications. I am not knocking that; if you have the faith, but I didn't have it.

One day I was out side washing and she was lying on the couch; which was after I got the Holy Ghost. You could not even tell she was breathing. I just couldn't stay out away from her long at a time, so I went inside to see about her. I just could not stand it anymore. I fell to my knees beside her and begged God to send me some help. A little while later Mama and my brother Charlie walked in. I told Charlie that my baby was dying, and to please help me. That night I went against Delbert and took her to the doctor. He sent her right on to the hospital; where they had to remove her tonsils. After that she was fine.

Maude and Delbert Massey
Paulette and Raymond circa 1949

5 OUR FAMILY

Delbert was bad to drink before God saved him. I didn't have much of a life then but he was always good to me, even though almost everything he made went on whiskey. He would get drunk and just knowing I was going to leave him would say, 'Girl, you are not going to leave me. If you get tired of living here we will move somewhere else.'
One night he got drunk and when he came in I was crying. I told him to go ahead and drink and go to hell because when I died I was going to heaven; although we were both lost as goats. He said, 'I'll tell you tonight and I'll tell you

again, tomorrow when I'm sober, if you go to heaven I'm going too, you are not going anywhere I can't go.'

Raymond was born April 12, 1949, and when he was six months there was a revival at the church nearby. At that time I had not even noticed the church being there.

The church had begun to fast and pray for revival in the community, and God began to move on my heart. I did not know what on earth was wrong with me, but I just knew I was fixing to die and I knew I was lost. They had a loud speaker outside of the church, and I could hear them all the way to my house and it was driving me crazy; I know now it was conviction. One Sunday my sister Evelyn and her husband came and spent the day with me. I asked her to come back that night and go to church with me. She said later, she really had no intentions of doing it but the later it got; the more miserable she got, so she came back and we went. This is an excerpt from a letter she wrote to Sue, March 23, 2001, sharing her version about taking me to church that night. It was about thirty five miles one way which made for a long round trip and it a school night and work day on Monday.

Dear Sue,
Maude said you would like for me to write about the time she first went to church at Midway. All my family and Mama went to spend Sunday with Maude. When we started to leave, she looked at me so sad looking and said, 'Evelyn, I wish you would come back and take me to that little ole church up there. I can hear the people praying and its driving me crazy.' So I said, 'Sure, I will', but decided not to. So, I started getting dressed to go to my own church, and I began to feel a heavy burden, and the later it got, the worse I felt and I said to myself, 'Foot, I'm not going to let this run me crazy. I'll go take her to church.'
When the people in church saw that she wanted to go; they took her next. Now the rest, she can tell you better than I can. But I wonder what would have happened to me if I had not gone back to take her there? Aunt Evelyn

It felt so good when I went to the altar, to lay that burden down. I will always be grateful to Evelyn for taking me to church that night.

We were not the first ones in our community to get in church. Delbert went with me the first night I went and when I went to the altar I just knew he would leave me; but I went anyhow. When I went outside he was standing out there talking to his old girlfriend. The devil sure knew how to work. Later our pastor said, he passed Delbert and me on the road one day and said to himself, 'It will take more than God to save those two.'

Delbert began to drink worse and I continued to go to church but I prayed more for him than I did for me. One evening we were sitting on the porch talking. I was ready to go to church and he would ask me about our friends, but he wouldn't ask about me. I still told him the preacher said, 'In heaven if we could see our loved ones in hell it wouldn't bother us. I believe it would hurt me to see you in hell even if I was in heaven.' He didn't say a word but the next evening he told me to get him some clothes, he was going with me.

Thank God for that day; it turned our lives around. He got the Holy Ghost before I did and from that time on church and God was our whole life; and still is mine today. I love the Lord with all my heart.

Delbert holding Raymond at six months old and Paulette standing in front of me. This is the day we were baptized in the precious name of Jesus

6 DELBERT'S HEALTH

When Sue was born January 31, 1951, it was freezing weather. I don't remember it ever being that cold before. Delbert went home to warm the house before he brought us home. After he left the house the line in the butane gas froze up and the house was full of gas fumes. He had to open the house up and let the gas fumes out and it gave me pneumonia; which lingered on until it developed into tuberculosis. I wasn't able then to do anything, and I had an awful cough. We heard about an evangelist holding a revival close by; so I made Delbert take me there. He didn't even know me but he called me out and prayed for me. God instantly healed me and the next day I did three weeks of laundry on our wringer washer.

Soon after that Delbert's health began to deteriorate. He lost so much weight it frightened me. He would hardly go to a doctor, but I talked him into going to Biloxi to the Veterans Administration Hospital, but it was almost too late. I fed him cracked ice all the way there and his mouth cracked and bled horribly. They soon diagnosed him with diabetes and then he went into a coma. I couldn't stay with him because I had just gotten over pneumonia and was still weak. That evening Daddy and me was setting on the front porch talking about the Pentecostal church and he told me, 'I don't believe in everyone praying at one time.' About an hour later Granny Lillie Massey and Delbert's brother Dewitt arrived and brought me a telegram from the VA hospital. It stated that Delbert was dying and had only a fifty-fifty chance of living and I was at liberty to visit him. There was a bunch of people there and I instantly fell down on my knees and went to praying. When I did everyone else did too. Before I got to the hospital, God had let me know that he was going to live. The doctors told Granny Lillie and me that they could not figure it out; but I could. Anyhow the very next evening Daddy and I were setting in the very same seat and I said, 'Daddy, I just want to ask you one question. Who led in prayer last night?' He had to agree there wasn't time to wait around when everyone prayed at the same time.

Sue was her daddy's sunshine but mean. Delbert loved all his children in their own special way. Once after my sister had cancer, she was at my house. When she got real nervous from the side effects of her cancer; she took nerve medicine that was prescribed for her. Only a half teaspoon would totally sedate her for hours; so when she took some we all went out of the house so we would not disturb her. Sue got hold of the bottle and drank almost the entire bottle.

Delbert had gone fishing and I had to rush her to the hospital. It was nip and tuck for a while but God brought her through.

One Sunday he had the children ready for a big day at church and we heard a big thud. Sue had pulled out the bottom drawer of a very heavy chest of drawers and climbed up on it. It fell on top of her; pinning her under it and hurting her so Delbert nailed the thing to the wall.

Donna Sue 1951

Sue was also very hard of hearing. I took her to an ear doctor and he said there was nothing that could be done to her hearing because it was from an un-natural, breech child birth. Later on the Lord healed her. She has always had lots of faith. One time we found she had taken a bunch of aspirins. We took her to the doctor but he determined she had not taken enough to hurt her. He just prescribed her a cone of ice cream that time.

After Delbert died Sue missed him so much too. I taught her the words to a song, 'How Far is Heaven,' which she learned and sang in church. I don't know who the writer is.

JESUS AND ME

How Far is Heaven

A little girl was waiting for her daddy one day,
It was time to meet him when she heard her mommy say,
Come to mommy darling, please do not cry,
Daddy's gone to heaven; a way up in the sky.

How far is heaven, when can I go,
To see my daddy he's there I know,
How far is heaven let's go tonight,
I want my daddy to hold me tight.

He was called so sudden that he could not say goodbye,
I know he's up in heaven, and we'll meet him by and by,
The little girl's lips trembled as she looked up in the sky,
And said Daddy's gone to heaven away up in the sky.

She just sung her heart out and never knew why everyone cried when she sang. She thought the line, "the little girl's lips trembled" was "the little girl's slip trembled" and sung it accordingly for a while.

Connie Jean 1952

When Connie was born May 9, 1952, I almost died then. My doctor walked out on me just moments before she was born because it was a very complicated case. Delbert got so angry and was going to beat him up but I told him not to; because God took care of us, and if the other doctor had stayed, we could have both died. She was very frail and sickly when she was small and for that reason she was my pet. I never could leave her for any reason. I guess I did a pretty good job of spoiling all of them. I spoiled them all then and still do today. I petted Raymond because he was my only son; and he is still very special and he knows it. Sometimes I just have a place in me that has to see or talk to him; then when I do I am all right for a while.

Before I finish this it will be very plain to see that God didn't make me rich; but he made a mother out of me. My children are next to God in my life. I can't stand for anyone to bother or talk about any of them or for anything to happen to any of them. I can say what I please; but everybody else, it is hands off. After all who else raised five perfect children? But when I got pregnant with Deb, I just wanted to die. Mine came so close together I was just tired of having babies. But before she was born I realized why God allowed them to come so closely. I couldn't do without any one of them. When I was pretty far along with her, Delbert's health began to really deteriorate at a fast pace due to his diabetes. His feet almost rotted off and he was fast becoming an invalid. He always told me that he had rather be dead than for me to have to make a living for him.

After he was diagnosed with diabetes he had to take insulin injections daily. One morning he opened the back door and threw his insulin as far as he could and he said, 'If God doesn't heal me, I'll be a dead man before long.' He also said, 'If I become unconscious, you will be the head of the house. If you let anyone bring me back, don't look for me until you see me coming, because I am going to get my part of this world until I die.' My blood ran cold because I knew he wouldn't be with me much longer.

7 MY PREMONITION

I begin to fast and pray; although I couldn't fast much due to my health and pregnancy but I almost prayed without ceasing. God began to deal with me and two weeks before he died his mother and I went to a funeral. While watching them load the corpse in the hearse something hit me and I said, 'That thing is coming to my house and it won't be long.' All that day I was lonely, blue and burdened. When I got home I begin to clean house and pray. All of a sudden I couldn't go any farther, so I fell down in the floor and said, "God, if you want him worse that I do, take him.' That was saying lots because I loved him so much. Two weeks from that day, I saw the hearse come to my house. Two weeks earlier I was ironing his clothes and my neighbor was visiting. I told her, 'I am ironing his clothes, but he will never wear them.' She said, 'Don't talk like that!' But God had spoken to my heart and he never wore them again.

Delbert loved me so and wherever we went he would slip up to me and say, 'Mrs. Massey, I love you.' That was also many times a day. When Paulette was born we slept with her and then when Raymond came along, Delbert took Paulette and slept in another room. Along about midnight I said aloud, 'I miss you,' and he answered back, 'Sugar, I miss you too,' and he come with Paulette. We slept with both children until Sue was born. I think he really knew he wasn't going to be around long, because he wouldn't even stay at work all day. He worked across the road from our house at the family business, Massey Lumber Company and came home at lunch for sure. He just wanted to be with his family. He was a praying man, and many times I would wake up and hear him praying for me especially and for his children. He begged God, "Hedge my children in from the things of the world, and I believe that they will make it." When he prayed the toes of his work boots marked the wood floor. When I sold the old place in 1988 and the owners removed the floor covering; those marks were still visible. They are a witness to his prayers.

Monday, October 18, 1953 was the last day I ever got him off to work. He went down very fast, even with me begging him to do something, but he wouldn't listen to me. He said, 'I had rather be dead than to be an invalid.' He also had many more health problems that he and I only knew about.

On Friday, October 23, 1953, my whole world fell apart. The one I loved on earth more than life itself died in my arms. I screamed, 'God, you have let me down!' I just could not stop screaming. Finally exhausted I fell down on my knees by the couch and God let me see him in a vision, just running from mansion to mansion. He was so happy and care free and I knew then it was the will of God, but what I couldn't understand was why God would take him from a twenty six year old, seven months pregnant woman, with four little ones? I think he had thirteen cents in his pocket and that was as far as I could see ahead. I didn't want to live and that was one time I didn't even want to live for my babies. I didn't see anything or any future.

I didn't know we had any life insurance but our insurance agent had kept his policy up that we thought had lapsed. My house was mortgaged also.

Somehow I got through the funeral believing that I would die when my baby was born. I think God let me believe that to keep me going. I made my brother guardian over my children so they would be taken care of. I went home with Mama after the funeral and slept as close to her as I could, but after that I went home to the loneliest place I have ever been in my entire life time. I didn't let my babies see how grieved I was. I made it until suppertime without breaking down, but when I sat down at the table; my heart broke and I fell down by a chair and cried my heart out. When I did all four little ones fell on me too and they began to cry. I knew then that they could never see me cry like that again, and they did not. But many have been the nights I wet my pillow thoroughly with my tears. I like to have never gotten over losing him. I realized I had to also stay away from his grave and until this day I can hardly go to his grave.

Being alone with five little ones; I was very scared. When it began to get dusk dark, I would stand and look out of the window and my little ones would ask, "Mother, what's the matter?" and I would tell them, "Nothing, I am just looking." I would be so scared I could not sleep at night but I never worried them with any of my problems. Mama and Daddy wanted me to live with them, but our ways was so different. I knew it wouldn't work out, but soon God took care of that. He took my fear and I wasn't afraid any more.

Maude holding Connie; Delbert with hand on Sue's head. Paulette standing beside Lillie Massey; Delbert's mother.

8 LIFE AFTER DELBERT

Delbert could not manage money and when he died he owed lots of bills. It took me a while to do it but I managed to pay the house off and all of his other debts. I dreamed one night he came back to me and I told him, 'You can come back but I will handle the money.' At his death I had an eighth grade education and no job or job skills. I didn't know which way to head, but I didn't spend much time feeling sorry for myself.

We drew Social Security and thanks to Mr. Dill, we had five thousand dollars insurance. I knew that in my grieved condition, I was in, I didn't need to draw it all out in a lump sum, so I asked for fifty dollars a month, and by doing so, I drew some interest on it, but that didn't give us enough to live on.

Maude and Deb in 1953

When Deb was born December 30, 1953, I faced another dark time. I was very sickly and had to face everything without Delbert. My sister Evelyn, who was a registered nurse, was really mad at me about Delbert's death. It so happened she was my nurse at Deb's delivery and as she gave me anesthesia, she would say repeatedly, 'Maude honey, breathe deep,' but it never knocked me out because I was having such a difficult delivery. When she left the hospital she went straight to Mama's and told her, 'Never worry about Delbert another day because Maude will never live to have another baby.'

I didn't want to live until they put my little baby in my arms, and oh, how I loved that little thing. I rocked her all the time, and would just lay awake at night and look at her.

When I took her home from the hospital, my cousin, came to see us. She was wealthy at that time and childless, and I was a widow with five children. She just knew I would give her my baby! She said,

'Just look, what we can give her that you can't.' I told her, 'I can give her a mother's love and you can't.' She and her husband was very well off but afterwards he died and she lost everything through bad management and died on welfare. Deb turned out much better off with me. I spoiled her then and she is still spoiled.

After my sister, died from cancer in 1955, Mama grieved really hard. My Daddy had never asked me for anything but he asked me to let Deb stay with Mama because he would hear Mama crying at night when Deb wasn't there; but if she had the baby she did not cry. It was the hardest sacrifice I ever made, so I started leaving her with Mama and Papa. That was a huge mistake because Mama was very worldly minded. I would teach Deb right and Mama would tear it down but they did both love her so much.

When Deb was six years old the doctor diagnosed her with tuberculosis. They had her in quarantined in a closed area in the hospital and wouldn't even tell me what was wrong. One morning the doctor let Evelyn, who was her nurse tell me her condition and it nearly killed me. But I began to fast and pray and one day I got Mama to stay with her and I went home fully intending to reach God. Sure enough, the next day, she went home and no tuberculosis; thank God.

SCHOOL DAYS 1962-63　LEAKESVILLE
Debra Faye Massey

MAUDE MASSEY

9 MAKING A LIVING JESUS AND ME

There is a hymnal whose lyrics record, 'Where Would I Be Without Jesus?' Well it is plain to see that my little family and I would have been in a mess, but my God walked so close to me then and does until this day. I couldn't begin to tell the times that God has healed me and my children. Not long after Delbert died, Deb was not born yet and Connie had a very high fever. Raymond was taking bronchial croup and I was so sick and tired. I just closed my eyes and prayed, "Lord, please let me go to sleep, and when I wake up let them be alright.' The next thing I knew it was morning and both of them was fine.

It took lots of money to raise that many children, but I always paid tithes and gave offerings. I also taught my children this at an early age. When I wrote my bills down and figured them up for the month, I never had enough money; but somehow I paid everything and had plenty to live on. No family around us had more than we did; God saw to that. One time I gave a special offering and didn't have enough to pay my bills when I had sent Paulette in the post office. While she was inside I looked in my wallet and there was money for my bills. God had put it there!

I worked awhile at the garment factory. When my sister was dying of cancer, she made me promise to take two of her oldest daughters and finish raising them. This now gave me seven children and about three hundred dollars a 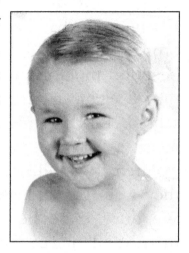 month income. Their dad did not help me one dime; so when I went to the factory, her daughters kept the children while I worked. They were good to the girls but not to Raymond and that just about worried me to death. I had contacted the Veterans Administration and was told several times that there was not benefits of any kind to help. So I only knew one thing to do and that was to fast and pray. This was one of the greatest miracles God ever performed for me that on the tenth day of my fast, I got a letter from the Veterans Administration that a law had been passed and signed by the President of the United States, Dwight Eisenhower that veteran's widows, and orphans of World War II would draw benefits monthly until the last child turned eighteen or graduated from high school. I had promised God, if He would make a way for me to be with my children, I would never leave them until they were big enough for me to do so. We drew these benefits until Deb got married. I never worked outside the home again until Deb was in school, then I drove a school bus for a while and in that way I could still be with them. This testimony has gone on to touch hundreds and today some are pastors and ministers of the gospel of Jesus.

When Delbert died Raymond was too little to help me with any chores, and we had a wood heater for heat. He would watch me cut wood with a big axe, and one day he said, 'Mother, when I get big you won't ever have to do that again.'

I use to get up before dawn and milk a cow before I went to work so we had plenty of milk and butter. I would put a calf on my cow and raise beef for the freezer. My brother Charlie and brother in law Jimmy Baygents always gave me vegetables for the freezer; so along with what I had planted, we had plenty of food.

When Sue was sixteen she developed a cyst on her back bone. When I took her to the doctor he made me feel and there was hard roots growing out from it. He told me that the roots had grown around into her backbone and spine and he really could not tell me it had not turned into cancer. When they operated on her I had already been fasting and praying and when the pathology report came back our family doctor; Doctor Raymond Tipton wouldn't even tell me the results; he make me read it myself and it read; 'Positively no malignancy,' thank my wonderful Lord.

10 GROWING FAMILY

My family began to grow and as the children began to marry, I never was ready to give one up so God just saw fit to give me some more. Paulette was the first to marry and even though Shelton never comes around he loves me and I do him too.

Viola is one of a kind; an endangered species and thank God she is mine. I have always treated her like my own daughters because that is how I feel about her. I could have picked the whole world over and never found better in-laws. God truly gave them to me. Graham was mine from the beginning; I picked him out. He has always been so special and good to me, I can't tell one bit of difference in him and Sue.

James was just another son. He liked to tease that I didn't want him and I didn't at first because I thought he would take my daughter to California; but he has made me proud of him. He was very good to Connie and James, Jr. He was a good person; a thankful person. He used to constantly tell me that he was more thankful for everything than he had been in his entire life. One of the greatest tragedies still that ever happened to our family was on September 19, 2004, when he was working on his tractor that Sunday; it turned over on him and killed him instantly. Connie has found happiness again and we are all so thankful for that because she really grieved over James. She met Russell Smith and they married and he is so good to her and James.

Deb's first marriage did not make it but sometimes some things can't be helped. Deb finally met and married Eddie Dueitt and he is wonderful. He is another one that was prayed down. Eddie is Graham's cousin and they are so much alike. It is amazing although they were not close how much they are alike.

Once when the FBI wouldn't leave Raymond alone, I prayed night and day. Another job I held at school was the dietician. I worked this job over thirty years until I retired. One day I was going around the county on my job and as usual I was praying for him. I was between Sand Hill and State Line, Mississippi schools, on a lonely road when I hit a little bird. I looked back and its little feathers were flying through the air. I began to weep, because I knew if God is mindful of that sparrow's fall; he is mindful of my son. I called him and told him, 'They will never bother you again,' and they didn't. Raymond and I have seen quite a few miracles. He depended on fireworks for a big portion of their income and this particular season, it was raining so much, he wasn't selling any fireworks at all. The weather forecast for the season was nothing but rain the entire time. He come and told me if the rain did not stop, he would lose money. I told him we would do something about that; and I began to pray. The next day, the sun was shining and he told his friend, 'Mother is praying!' It did not rain another drop on them until they closed at midnight New Years night. Going home it rained on them. That was God letting him know what He could do. There were other times like that when God stopped the rain on their fireworks season.

Raymond became an alcoholic and went pretty far out in sin. One night I was praying for him and God impressed me, 'Give him to me, and pray for someone else.' For about two years I didn't pray for him but I would praise God for what He was going to do. About six months later, he called and told me, he was delivered from alcohol; oh praise my wonderful and mighty God! He is now going to church. He's not there yet, but he is on his way. I have asked God to save me, and mine regardless of the cost.

That's saying a mouthful but anything beats a lost eternity.

Maude Massey with children, Raymond, Sue, Connie and Paulette circa 1960's

My children have always come to me when they have problems; and as they depend on me, I depend on God. We have prayed for sick animals, ball games, ailing horses; lost dogs, boyfriend problems, you name it, and we have took it to God and still do, but I have never seen a problem too great or too small that my God can't handle.

After Deb divorced, we saw some trying times. She was going down the wrong side of the road. I knew if God didn't move her life would be ruined, so every morning at six o'clock, another prayer partner and me was in the church praying. Only Deb and I will ever know all the problems, but God let me know one morning that he was going to move for a certain request; and I asked God to confirm it to her. She said, she was standing in front of her sink and something washed over her from her head to her feet. I thought it was going to happen right then but it didn't happen for so long. I was about to lose hope and just like always, it happened and only

God could have moved as clearly; right Deb? God has moved, for her and Eddie so many times since they have been married. Poor Eddie in the shape he was in, only God could have so completely straightened things out in his life.

MAUDE MASSEY

11 HEALTH AND MIRACLES

Faith in God is the most wonderful gift a person could ever have. I believe I have that gift or maybe there was no alternative. I had no work experience and no education when Delbert died. But I soon went to work and got my diploma and went to trade school and took typing classes that helped on my jobs. I also drove to Mobile nights and took schooling as a florist. I made extra income doing weddings, and other floral business. I was working in the school cafeteria and I have always done my very best on any job I had. Our principal at that time, began to notice how I worked and asked me if I would like to go to the annex as a manager, and I certainly did. Not long after that he gave me two schools to supervise.

Our superintendent of education at that time, appointed me to Greene County Supervisor over the entire county. God richly blessed me with the ability to do this job. I worked there thirty two years. I worked when people were looking for jobs everywhere. I have never known what it was not to bring home a payday. I can not tell you it was easy; but I can tell you that God was with me ever step of the way.

Sometime in 1982, I developed heart trouble. I would not let my children know how sick I was but there were many nights I did not sleep. Finally I went to a heart specialist and he put me on an all night monitor; then he was going to send me on to a hospital. After I left his office I got to thinking about it. My granddaughter Kathy Pierce went with me, and we were going to spend the night at Sue and Grahams house. I told her not to tell Sue but go in her back bedroom, and call the doctor and tell him, I want to cancel the appointment and monitor. Kathy called and the nurse told her if I had a heart attack, I could not sue them; and Kathy said I did not intend to do that. I began to pray about my condition, and my pastor at that time, called me out one night and prayed for me, and God healed me sound and well. That is just another miracle of many in my life.

I took a bad case of the flu in 1988. I don't recall ever being that sick in my whole life. Just as I felt I was about to recover, I would relapse. About this time I started going through one of the hardest trials I have faced since Delbert died. I fought this trial for at least six months. Just as I was about to totally give up; God released me from it. I have never understood what it was all about, but when I got victory over it, God gave me a closer walk and greater desire than I have ever had before. I truly realize, as the hymnal lyrics say, 'There is Nothing, No Nothing, That my God can't do.'

One Friday night I had company and we was setting around talking. All of a sudden a burden begins to roll over me, and I felt like I had to pray! I ask her if she too had ever felt like she had to pray. We sat there a few more minutes and finally I told her, I had to pray; and we did. The next morning which was a Saturday, I told my granddaughter Donna, I was going to Lucedale; something I never did. I worked all week and loved to stay home on Saturday because that was also my only day to work at home. I did not intend to; but we went to another store and the nearer we got, we could see a wreck. The ambulance was there and people crowded around it. We too, begin to push through the crowd and Donna said, 'Granny, it is a blue truck that has a rebel tag on the front of it!' To my shock it was Graham and my grandson Eddie. They took them both to the hospital and thank God, neither were hurt; but what was so odd;

was that Sue stayed home to clean house when she usually always goes with them. The truck was totaled and I know now but for prayer the night before; they could have been killed. I knew what my burden was all about. What a mighty God we serve!

Graham Crocker behind the truck that was totaled

Sue Massey Crocker wrote the following testimony of a miraculous answer to Maude's prayers in 2004:

Not only have we seen the results of Mother's prayers and then heard testimonies of mother's prayers reaching Jesus but there are other miracles we know of her praying about. It dominated world and national news when a truck driver named Tommy Hamill from Mississippi, who was working in Iraq, was captured April 9, 2004. His captors threatened to kill him unless the United States lifted its siege on Fallujah. This led the news for several weeks because so many other hostages that had been kidnapped like him had been executed by their captors. Never have we ever known of anything in the news affecting mother the way this did. Being a mother this really touched her and like so many others all over the world she really prayed for him. She does not claim to be the one who reached God for him; but we knew that for days mother really had a burden for him as if he was her own son.

One Sunday night after praying over into the night she felt peace about him. She called me the following day and asked if there was any way that I could find out this man's address because she wanted to send the family a card. She said, 'This morning, I was down by my bed praying for him at two o'clock and the Lord spoke to me, 'they are not going to kill him; Tommy Hamill is coming home safely.' She wanted also to let his family know a mother from Lucedale, Mississippi is praying for Tommy. I did find the information she wanted on the internet and called it back to her and she immediately mailed her letter to the family. Sure enough he was released.

The following Sunday morning I was sick and did not go to church. Mother called to check on me before going to Sunday night service. In the course of our conversation I asked what she thought of the latest news about the man from Mississippi. She said, 'No I don't know; what about it?' I felt sure she of all people would know that sometime after midnight there was a breaking bulletin on the news that stated, 'Mississippi man escapes Iraqi captors alive, in US military protection!' When I told her about it, she just started saying, 'Praise you Jesus! I knew they would not kill him and that he would come out of this ordeal alive because I asked God to dispatch angels all around him. There is no way they could touch him.' When she got to church that night she told a few people about it and word got to the pastor. He asked her to give her testimony to the whole church about what the Lord had done. Later, while reading the paper, there was an article about an interview given by the mayor of the city he is from that said, "After we had gotten news of Tommy's release when I got back to my office, there was a note left on my desk that was written by one of our policemen that read, 'The Lord spoke to me in prayer, Tommy is coming home!" Praise Jesus; he heard our mother's prayers for someone else's child.

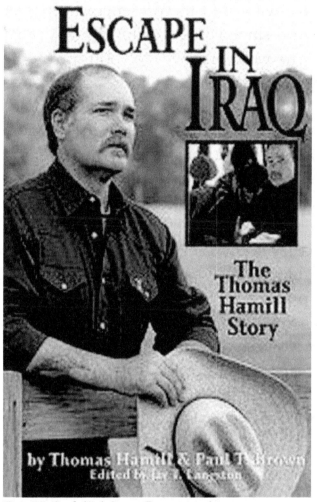

B&H Publishing Group, Amazon.com, Barnes&Noble.com, Books-A-Million, IndieBound, Library

I have witnessed the presence and power of God since I was a child. I know what it is to walk on the very bottom of the valley; and I also know about the mountain top. I know what it is to see my child go to the bottom and watch God pull them out. I have watched and prayed as it seemed that the devil had won the battle as one of them would walk out into the world. But no matter how far they went they could never get past the blood of Jesus Christ and the power of prayer. Jesus always won the battle then and now.

Everyone always wonders why I have never remarried. One reason was that I spent the short years I was married hurting. Delbert and I was married only three days and the army separated us almost two years then I had to give him up after only eight years of marriage. I knew if I never loved again; I would never have to hurt like that again.

Another reason is my five little hearts. I couldn't have stood for any man to lay a hand on them. I have loved and protected them all these years. I can take anything except having someone mess with one of them; that makes the wildcat come out in me.

MAUDE MASSEY

12 GRANDCHILDREN MIRACLES

I guess of all the proud Grannies; I must be the proudest. I could write a whole book about just them. I love them all so very much and try not to play favorites with them but I do try also to be there for the one that needs me most.

When my grandson Eddie Crocker was in four year kindergarten, I began to worry about him. I prayed and prayed for him one particular morning. My secretary had left the office and I looked at his picture on my desk in his little cowboy suit and I began to pray, 'God please don't let anything happen to him.' For some reason I felt such an urgency to pray for him and did.

It was April 11, 1977 and Sue called me with the news. She said, 'Our neighbor was killed on the way back from taking Eddie and his daughter to kindergarten this morning.' I said, 'Oh my God, Sue! That wreck was meant to be going to kindergarten but God spared him.' I have a picture of him standing by the totaled truck.

Eddie Crocker at four looks over the truck he was passenger in that claimed the life of the driver.

JESUS AND ME

Eddie and the little blue cowboy suit

When Connie's son, James, Jr., was in the second grade, he was terrified of his teacher. I decided to visit his class room and check it out; since I had a good relationship with all the teachers in the county. When I got to the room, he was just rigid, looking straight ahead. The teacher could not understand it. I dreamed that they had shut him up in a room and would not let me get to him. Boy that next morning I went to see her and told her that she was the best teacher in our school but our baby was horrified of her. I told her to hug our baby and she did. That evening he ran all the way home from the bus to their store and said, 'Mama, I don't know why I was scared of her. I sure hope she is my teacher next year.' I would take him to school daily and pick him up if the weather was bad. He would sit on the arm rest; what we called the buddy seat. He was sick lots and one evening he was lying in the back of the store. I knelt down and said, 'Lord, touch my baby.' Very quickly he looked up at me and said,

'Granny, don't ever do that at school.' He was afraid I was going to come in his room and pray for him! When Gene, Clint, Sherry and Kim attended one of the schools I supervised I made sure they got extra milk and food if they wanted it.

I always tried to see to all of them. One day my state supervisor came and we started at one school and made the rounds to all of them; I would show her my grandchildren and she could not believe I had that many grandchildren. Pete was in special education. One day I walked by and looked in on him and he looked so sad. I went by Paulette's house on the way home and told her to take him out of that mess and she did.

Robby's hip bone deteriorated when he was about three years old and he had to use crutches for a long time. I use to watch out my kitchen window at him trying to run with the other children on crutches. I would cry until the tears would pour down my neck. Through prayer; God completely healed him.

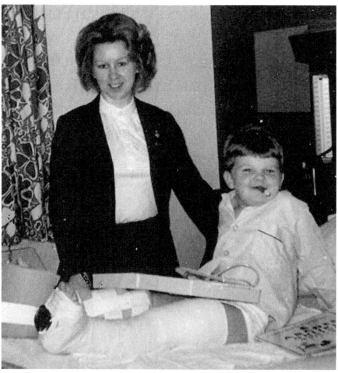

Rob Burnett and Aunt Sue Crocker December 1979

Another grandson, Clint wanted to go to college and did not have the money. I pulled strings and got him the college bus to drive so he could go. Between all of us we all prayed Eddie Crocker and James Jr., through college and believe me I still pray for them.

After I retired June 30, 1992, all of the children had married and left home so Deb and Eddie bought the Jiffy Mart; a store they still run today. I was left alone so I sold my house in Greene County and built an apartment onto her and Eddie's house. I cannot be treated any better. Eddie is like my own child and I think he feels the same about me. I told him and Graham when their own mother's died that I would be there for them and I am.

Delbert told me before he died to stay at our house and raise our family and I did until they were all grown and gone. I have never missed the old place because I had too hard of a time there and it became too much for me to keep up.

13 SHOULDER SURGERY

In February 1999, Paulette had gotten her a job and I did not know that she was having such a hard time. One day I was shopping and one of the ladies from her church was there and told me that she had picked Paulette up walking to work. That hurt me so badly and I went to praying about it.
As I begin to read my Bible it came to a portion of scripture where it reads, 'Jesus passed by.' Boy that jumped out at me and I said, 'Lord, when you pass by everything will be all right.' I just buried my face in my Bible and gave it all to Jesus. I called Eddie and asked if he

knew of a car she might be able to get; and he told me someone to talk to. I told him my problem and he did have a used Thunderbird he would let me have for five hundred dollars. I said, 'Sold!' I called Raymond and he said he would put two hundred dollars in the mail to go towards it. Deb handed me two hundred dollars and I put the rest and we bought it for Paulette. Ina filled it up with gas and Sue and Graham bought the tag. I called Paulette and asked if she could come and pick up her car; and praise the Lord in less than an hour, 'Jesus passed by,' and she did not walk another time.

It may not mean much to anyone else but it meant the world to Raymond. His dog that he loved like his own child died. We all prayed for her but when she died, I began to pray that Jesus would give him peace about it. Later he told me that he felt perfect peace over it. That is our God! I never question Jesus but sometimes you can't help but wonder. I watched as others got prayers answered and yet could do things that weren't according to the Bible. One night I was praying and I asked God about it. Like a light from heaven it came to me, 'There is a way that seemeth right unto a man, but the end there of are the ways of death.' After that, I will never question my God again.

I truly feel like we are living in the midnight hour. Many times I tell Jesus, 'I know that you are not coming tonight, because all of my babies are not ready.' I hold to that promise; as surely as God promised Abraham, Isaac and Jacob; He promised me because I raised my babies after Jesus.

In late 2000 I fell in church and tore the rotator cuff loose in my shoulder. In February 2001 I had surgery on it. Sue and Deb had asked the doctor if he could fix it. He said that at my age he might not have anything to work with. One of our local pastors was there for my surgery, and he said when the doctor came out after my surgery to speak to my family, he said, 'I had everything I needed to work with.' Sue had sent him a prayercloth and my testimony and it really touched him. He even wrote her a letter thanking her for it.

In August after five months, I went back and he told me my arm was freezing up and he would most likely have to put me to sleep and break it loose. I was really suffering with it. He and the therapist had told me I would never get full use of my arm again. I had another appointment three weeks later and I promised God if he would heal me I will testify to the doctor about it.

On Sunday morning before that appointment the preacher was teaching Sunday School and the power of Jesus was moving. Suddenly he stopped and said, 'I could go on with this lesson, but somebody needs prayer,' and I knew it was me. I stepped out and they prayed for me and praise Jesus, I was healed instantly! I went back for my appointment and when the doctor came in he said, 'Well, how are you today?' I said, 'Why don't I show you.' I lifted both my arms up and he did not know what to think. He asked, 'What in the world has happened to you?' I said, 'The Great Physician has healed me.' He could not believe what he was seeing.

In the middle of the year 2000 I was going to mid-week service because I never missed church. The radio had weather advisories that predicted heavy, dense fog. I wanted so badly to go to church and I did not have anyone to go with me, so I went anyway. After church was over as I drove out of the church parking lot, I could hardly see my own car for the fog. I began to pray for protection when I noticed a little white car had pulled out of a side road. As I drove behind it, I could see perfectly. As we both came to a turn the little car turned the same way that I was going. It also made three other turns, each one going the same way that I was going. We drove nine miles and the little car came right to my door; and I never saw it again.

God sent an angel to guide me safely home. Just another testimony; thank you Jesus.

14 BURDEN FOR BOBBIE JO

In April 2003, I dreamed of my niece Barbara 'Bobbie Jo' Williams Turner that I had not seen nor heard from in years. I had a very heavy burden for her. I dreamed that I went to see her and told her the Plan of Salvation. Sue knows me well; so when I told her about my dream and how burdened I was for Bobbie, she started searching for her on the internet and found her living in Bay Minette, Alabama. Sue contacted her and told her that she was bringing me to see her. She was so happy to hear from us. She cooked lunch for us and after we had eaten I shared my dream with her. I told her that I had brought my Bible and felt to explain to her; the Plan of Salvation; and I did.

As I was sharing my thoughts with her, she just ate it up. She said, 'Aunt Maude nobody has ever told it to me like that before; I see it.' Sue and I prayed for her and she came back to the Lord right there in her living room. Since then she has really been blessed and totally lived for God until her death in 2009. She would call me lots of times to let me know what God had done for her and her family through prayer. She said, 'Aunt Maude, if it had not been for you and my pastor, I would be lost. If I make it to heaven it will be because of you.'

Thank God for my dream, or Bobbie would have been lost.

JESUS AND ME

Barbara 'Bobbie Jo' Williams Turner

Barbara Turner and I after prayer. There are tears still on her cheeks from praying.

15 JESUS STAYS THE STORMS

In January 2006 my other arm went bad on me. Doctor McAndrews said that I had to have surgery on it. Somehow Deb could not stand for me to have that surgery and kept putting it off. Our pastor was preaching one night and stopped and said, 'Sister Massey, the devil has afflicted your body and it is going to be all right.' Instantly my arm was healed. Deb told me later that the devil is going to have to slip up on you to kill you because God always heals you. Jesus can do anything!
He said in His word, 'I know your name, and in another place I will help you.' He

even numbers the stars and calls them each by their own name. How could I ever doubt Jesus? He is my Savior, my lover, my best friend, my King of all Kings and Lord of Lords. He is with me in the valleys, in the high places and the low places and I worship and love Him beyond words.

On July the ninth of two thousand five; hurricane Dennis was forecasted to come our way. It was a category four storm and coming right at us. Deb and I was praying about it; when a minister called me and gave me a message in tongues. He said, 'Be not afraid for I am in the midst.' We both knew that it would not hit us; instead it hit Florida. We did not even get much rain from it; praise our Jesus.

In mid March of 2006, I went to bed and a burden fell on me so heavily. I cried, prayed and hugged my Bible for a very long time before I came through it. The next morning I told Deb that I prayed something off somebody in my family last night. Two days later Connie called me and told me that Russell almost got killed. He had fallen off a building scaffold but he caught something before he hit the ground. Something went all over me and I told her about my burden; I knew that is what it was about and Jesus had intervened.

On December 18, 2006, I was alone when I wrecked my car and totaled it out. Since I got the Holy Ghost I have not cut my hair in over 60 years. I gave Jesus my hair then and have always felt my uncut hair is my Godly covering. I had enough presence of mind to give Sue's phone number. When the lady behind me that witnessed my wreck called Sue she told her, 'I was screaming as her car was spinning around. Her head was shaking violently back and forth like a rag doll. She is certain to have either a broken neck or serious head and neck injuries.' Later one of the high patrol officers was describing it to my family and told them it was the same type of accident that instantly killed a race car driver. My hair was pinned up and as my head was thrown around; my uncut hair was falling down around me.

When authorities arrived, I was already out of the car unhurt! I did not even take an aspirin for pain. I had a few bruises. Everywhere my hair fell around me I was protected because my glory, covering and covenant sustained me! A few months prior to my wreck God began to deal with me for a closer walk with Jesus.

I can truly say I have never been as close to God as I am now for that very reason. The enemy tried again to kill me. About a week before the wreck, Deb and I was passing a carwash in Lucedale when a big truck passed us and a two by four blew off it and totally splintered. If it had hit our windshield it would have killed us both but the angels of Jesus encamp around them that fear Him.

I do fear the Lord but I also love Him with all my whole heart. I knew that angels were in that car with me because the entire front was bashed in.

I have lived for Jesus over six decades and I do not cut my hair. Therefore I have power with the angels because of my uncut hair. Some time ago Deb was in so much pain.

I went to prayer that night fully intending to reach Jesus for her. I caught my head on each side and came boldly to the throne of Grace and prayed, 'Jesus, if I have power with the angels, send one to her now.' The next morning she was fine. Jesus never fails a promise.

MAUDE MASSEY

16 MEETING JENNIFER

In May of 2007 Graham had to have triple bypass. Eddie was working in Valdosta, Georgia and was so worried about his dad; and he was alone too much. It was the hardest thing in the world for him to drive off and leave his dad so sick. He was also worried about the load Sue was under and wanted so badly to be at home but he just could not find a job at all closer by.
I began to pray for Eddie to be able to come home and that a good job would open up for him. He had finally made the decision to just quit and come home; when Graham had told him not to be too

hasty with his resignation. I was praying and he was thirty minutes away from turning in his two weeks notice; when his boss called him in and laid him off. Not only was he able to come home but he was able to draw unemployment, and given severance pay and other great benefits. God also opened the door and he got a better job at home making a better salary.

I posted the date as November 18, 2009 but not sure of the exact time. But Jennifer Parker; our little angel with broken wings was still living in Florence, South Carolina. She and Eddie had not yet married and she was having tormenting episodes of kicking and jerking until she could not sleep and was so sleep deprived. Deb and I were shopping when Sue got news to us that Jennifer was very sick and asked us to stop wherever we were and agree in prayer for her. It so happened we had stopped for lunch and we immediately caught hands and begin to pray.

Later we got home and I was still concerned for Jennifer. She is more like me than my own children. I was just walking through my house and praying when the spirit of the Lord fell on me. I felt instantly to go to my door and rebuke the spirit of the enemy out of Jennifer's house. I came in my living room and opened my door and said, 'Devil, this is Jennifer's door. I am commanding you in JESUS name to go!' I suddenly felt that spirit of darkness move from her life and home.

Later on I called and checked on her and told her what I had felt to do on her behalf. At that very instant; Jennifer had felt to go to her door and do the same thing I had done hundreds of miles away. What a mighty God we serve! As I had my hand on my door for her in Mississippi; she had her hand on her door in South Carolina praying the same prayer and she has not been bothered with that spirit again.

Jennifer is very special to me in a way no one else is. I prayed many nights for Jesus to put someone in Eddie Crocker's life when God gave him the very best; a little girl full of the Holy Ghost and baptized in Jesus name.

I wish Mama and Daddy could have met Jennifer and Eddie. This picture is the way I really remember Mama and Daddy. The wedding band Mama has on her finger in this picture is the one Jennifer wears today. She gave it to Sue when she married Graham.

Mama and Daddy really loved Graham. The first time Sue took him to meet them Daddy nearly embarrassed her to death. He would always save all his change for my children when they were small. When they left he would divide it up between the five of them. So when Graham and Sue left, he gave Graham a quarter and him a college graduate and working at the shipyard making good money. Graham says today he wish he had kept that quarter.

Jennifer Crocker and Granny Maude
2010

17 TEST OF FAITH

I believe that the year 2009, was one of the hardest I have ever faced. In March one night I went to bed with a burden. I began to pray and worship the Lord all night and if I dozed off, I still worshipped. About five o'clock in the morning my Lord gave me a song by the Crabb family and some of the lyrics were, 'Hold On, I'll take you Through the Fire Again.' I did not know what it was at the time, but I soon found out God was getting me ready for a trial that lasted a year.

I was in my garden one day and something spoke to me, 'I am soon to take you home.' For a while the enemy tried to torment me about it. Finally I rebuked that spirit in Jesus name, and said, 'Jesus, take me, I am ready; this is why I have lived for you all these years.' That spirit left me and did not bother me again. Two weeks after that Sue, Deb and I were in my living room. I told them, 'The strangest thing happened to me two weeks ago and since you girls are here I want to tell you. The Lord spoke to me that He is soon to take me.' They looked at each other and then Sue and Deb shared something with me that happened a couple weeks earlier.

This is Sue's experience and the dream she had.

April 18, 2009 was mother's eighty second birthday; we all took her out to eat then my family and I came home. It should have been a festive time; but for some reason I was very troubled in my spirit. We read the Bible and prayed as a family like we do nightly and finally went to bed. I am a person that God has always dealt with in dreams and around two the next morning I was awakened by a disturbing dream.

I dreamed of being at a body of water with other people. I could hear Bible verses being quoted, "Come away my love, my fair one, my turtle dove, my dove" etc; then in the distance I could hear a song written by Governor Jimmie Davis, 'I Dreamed I Bowed on My Knees and Cried Holy.' I could see upstream there was some kind of ledge where water flowed over it and ran down stream. Later I looked across the bank to the East side and could see a person that just suddenly appeared out of a mist but I did not know who it was. Then everything was quiet. After the words and singing stopped I realized some other people were there and I asked, 'Who is that on the other side and what are they doing here?' Someone answered, 'Honey don't you know? That is your dad; he has come to take your mother across Jordan.'

I was so troubled that I got up to pray and read my Bible. As I was opening it; it fell open to the Song of Solomon to the exact words in my dream. Graham came in the living room and asked me what was wrong and if I was praying and I told him, 'I have just had a dream.' He asked, 'is it good or bad; do you want to tell me about it?' I told him, 'I don't know why but for some reason I am troubled for mother because I have just had a dream that God is going to take her.'

Since our dad died mother has missed him so much that nearly six decades later she has never cared to even date another man. Her face still lights up like a teenager or young love when she talks about him. Mother always says, 'When I get to heaven I want to see Jesus first then Delbert.' Sometime after his death a lady told mother in prophecy, 'Sister Maude you have been so faithful to God and when you die God is going to let Brother Delbert be your death angel.' My aunt and another lady mother once went to church with had also told me this too.

When I was awakened by that dream I was greatly disturbed and suddenly started thinking about the song, 'I

Dreamed I Bowed on My Knees and Cried Holy.' I have heard this song all my life but only had heard two stanzas never knowing there is a third.

I Bowed on My Knees and Cried Holy.

Verse 1: I dreamed I went to a city called glory oh so bright and so fair
When I entered the gate, I cried holy; the angels all met me there
They showed me from mansion to mansion and oh the sights I saw
But I said, I want to see Jesus; the One who died for all.
Verse 2: I thought when I entered that city, my friends all knew me well.
They showed me all thru heaven, the scenes are too numerous to tell.
They showed me Abraham, Isaac and Jacob, Mark, Luke and Timothy,
But I said, I want to give praise, to the One who died for me.
CHORUS: Then I bowed on my knees and cried holy, holy, holy,
I clapped my hands and sang glory, glory to the Son of God.

But in my dream I could hear a third verse.

Verse 3: I thought when I saw my Savior, Oh! Glory to God!
I just fell right down before Him,
Singing, "Praise to the name of the Lord."
I bowed down and worshipped Jehovah, my friend of Calvary
For I wanted to give praise to Jesus, for saving a sinner like me.

Later when I researched old hymnals I found the third verse.
It was Sunday morning and I called my sister Deb and told her what I dreamed and said, 'Deb I don't know how to tell you this but God is fixing to take Mother and soon!' After I told her my dream and what I experienced she said, 'You know I am sitting here fixing my hair for church and I thought; I feel like I am fixing my hair for mother's funeral.'

I did not say anything to mother because I did not know how to tell her what I knew was a message from God. The following Saturday we went to mother's and Deb and I was with her in her house. She said, 'Since I have you two girls here I want to tell you what happened to me. I was in my garden two weeks ago and the Lord spoke to me that I am going to take you.' I told her, 'Mother if you had not said that I would not tell you about the dream I had that I shared with Deb last week.' Then I proceeded to tell Mother what I had dreamed. It also turned out that Paulette, Connie and Raymond had the same feeling too.

As I was telling it, she began to pick it up and tells the same thing herself! She told us that when Daddy died she was seven months pregnant with Deb and when she knew he was gone that she began running. She did not know where, she just ran. As she was praying and asking God why He took Daddy she began to hear the song, 'I Bowed On My Knees.' She could hear the lyrics;

They showed me from mansion to mansion and oh the sights I saw, but I said I want to see Jesus; the one who died for all.

We never knew this about the song having such a place in her life.

Mother was scheduled for a colonoscopy on Memorial Day; May 25th several weeks after my dream. At first I started not to go with her and Deb because it was just a routine procedure but changed my mind and went. When they concluded her procedure they told us they had found a golf ball size tumor in her colon and recommended she be admitted to the hospital immediately to schedule surgery, because doctors was absolutely certain it was malignant. Seven doctors came in to see her for various reasons and all seven was certain of one thing; she had cancer. We were just devastated! The surgeon even told her they would do chemo treatments just to be sure there would not be cancer cells that had been missed and that the most side effects if any would be hair loss. Mother looked at the doctor and pointed her finger at him and said, 'I gave my hair to Jesus over sixty years ago and I will not lose it to chemo. God can take me!' He patted her on the leg and said, 'We'll see.'

Deb and I have discussed many times about the passage in the Bible of Elijah and his mantle and the passing of it to Elisha. We declare our mother's mantle will go to us. My family and I set aside 'prime time' at our house for reading the Bible and prayer every night. We started at the first and reading the Bible through and you might know that night it would be about Elijah and his mantle! I always read but this night I could not; Eddie did. May 27th was the day of her surgery and it was the hardest thing I have faced knowing what I had dreamed. We felt peace but still this dream still lingered in my mind. There were so many people there for her and before going to surgery with her and the family to the waiting area we all gathered in her room and prayed. There were hundreds of people that called, visited, emailed and texted when the news about mother was known. They came to get mother and were taking her to surgery and told us to go to the surgery waiting area. We were going down a glass windowed corridor to the surgery waiting area, when we turned the corner I looked to my left and I just broke down weeping. There was that body of water that I saw in my dream and there was a ledge extending from its banks on the east side! The only difference was, in the dream, there was nothing on the banks; no hospital or other buildings. It ran east and west and on the east side is where my dad stood. Everyone else was composed but I was weeping. Finally, one of the ministers I had shared my dream with looked at me and said, "That's the body of water you saw in your dream isn't it?" I just shook my head yes; there was even the ledge on the eastern side where daddy stood in my dream.

Body of water in my dream seen at the hospital.

We fasted and prayed as never before that if it be the will of God to spare her life, to give her a quality life. Mother came through her surgery and she did not have cancer! Doctors told us that most people her age never get back on their feet again. Later they said it would take at least twenty weeks because of her age to recover. Praise Jesus; her hospital stay was only nine days. Two weeks later she was cooking and three weeks later she was back in church and buying her own groceries. It has just been one miracle after another for her and we give praises to the name of Jesus! Not only did she not have cancer but she has lived to see a fifth generation born in our family.

This is not the first we have seen her come through. After I married she was not feeling well and I took her to a doctor. He kept her for hours and then called me in for conference. He said he had gone back through her entire life and told me, that what our mother went through and had to face losing our dad should have killed her. He said that watching him die being so young with small children was such a traumatic experience that unknowingly around the time daddy got sick until his passing every year she begins to relive everything. Today we know it as post traumatic stress syndrome and many are never the same. We all honor her highly. There is a song that could have easily been written just for her from all of us called, "Give Mother My Crown." We don't know who the writer is:

MAUDE MASSEY

Give Mother My Crown

*She's labored so hard in the world below,
And didn't have the things most mothers know,
Feeding us children on a widows small pay,
Washing and ironing since dad passed away.
I want to go to heaven when this life is o'er,
To be with Jesus on eternity's shore,
But if I've a crown coming when rewards go around,
Please blessed Jesus give mother my crown.
I didn't realize it just being a child,
Just how great of burden my mother had,
Adoption was offered, but she just said no,
Instead she taught us the right way to go.*

In Maude's words:
On May 25, 2009 I had to go for a colonoscopy when they found a mass the size of a golf ball in my colon. Doctors felt it was so urgent; they would not even let me leave the hospital because I needed surgery. Prior to surgery, my primary care doctor and six other specialists told me they judging from their experience, they were all positive that I had colon cancer and furthermore they all agreed that I would also have to take chemo. They also did a CT scan on my liver because that is the first organ colon cancer attacks around the tumor. When I was told that one of the side effects of treatment would be losing my hair; I refused to take it and lose my Godly covering; my uncut hair. My family, friends, church and I started praying for God to intervene for my situation.

I had colon surgery on May 27, 2009 and they removed the tumor and several inches of my colon. When my surgeon met with my family afterwards; he told them I came through my surgery fine but would be later getting cancer results. I was told that at my age, which was eighty two at that time, I could be as much as twenty weeks recovering from this type of surgery and facing weeks in the hospital. Furthermore, they told me I would be at least a couple months before I would feel like resuming any activities I enjoyed prior to surgery.

There was not one favorable bit of information I was given; everything was so discouraging. Little did they know what the great physician knew. I spent only five days in the hospital. On Sunday, June 7th, I made an entry in my journal, 'Today is eleven days since my surgery and I have cooked Sunday dinner for my family.' I not only cooked for my family but three weeks later I was back in church and buying my own groceries! When I went back to the doctor to get the staples removed the surgeon said, 'Lady, you are a testimony. You do not have cancer.' What a mighty Jesus we serve. There is power in the blood of the Lamb.

When I did suffer with my stomach, I called my doctor and asked for something to give me relief. He said that I would have to live with that condition for the rest of my life; that was just part of it. But there again, my God has touched my body and I am eighty four years old and can do most anything I want to do. Jesus brought me through the fire once again.

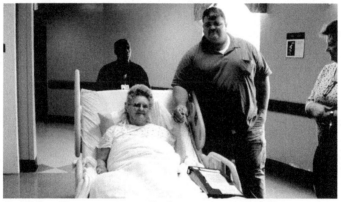

Robby Burnett and Granny Maude on way to surgery

18 I DON'T REGRET A MILE

February 25-26th, 2009: I went to bed so completely discouraged about the worldliness that has been allowed to come into our churches that our church leaders are condoning. I had made up my mind to quit going to the church I was attending. I tried to read my Bible and I just could not get my mind on it. I felt there was no use to even pray because my mind was so confused. But I began to pray and God covered me up with His spirit. For over an hour I wept and poured out my heart to my God. I begged Him to give me direction. I prayed most of the night and at about five o'clock in the morning God sang me a song by the Crabb family entitled:

*Don't Give Up; Hold On;
I'll Take You Through the fire again.'*

*So many times I've questioned certain circumstances and things I could not understand. And many times in trials, weakness blurs my vision that's when my frustration gets so out of hand.
It's then I am reminded: that I've never been forsaken I've never had to stand one test alone. When I look at all my victories and the spirit rises up in me and it's through the fire my weakness is made strong!
He never promised that the cross would not get heavy and the hill would not be hard to climb.
He never offered our victories without fighting but He said help would always come in time.
So just remember, when you're standing in the valley of decision and the adversary says "give in",
Just hold on, My Lord will show up
And He will take you through the fire again!*

I know now that I have to hold on for my family as well as for some of the church people that are trying so hard. I will never forget the closeness I had all night with my wonderful Jesus. I worship Him with my whole heart and I will turn the church over to him. Only one time in almost sixty years that I have lived for the Lord that I had this same experience and it is awesome. I don't regret a mile; I've traveled for the Lord.

I Don't Regret a Mile

I don't regret a mile
I've traveled for the Lord,
I don't regret a time
I've trusted in his word,
I've seen the years go by
Many days without a song,
But I don't regret a mile
I've traveled for the Lord.

I've dreamed many dreams that have never come true and I've seen them vanish at dawn;

MAUDE MASSEY

*But I've realized enough of my dreams thank
God, to make me want to keep dreaming on.
I've got up out of bed many times at the midnight
hour to pray a prayer that seemed no answer
would come to,
Though I waited patiently and long,
But answers have come to enough of those prayers
to make me want to keep praying on;
I've trusted many a friend that's failed me and
left me to weep alone,
But I've found enough of those friends to be true
blue to make me keep trusting on.
I've sowed a many seed that's fell by the wayside
for the birds to feed upon,
But I've held enough golden sheaves in my hand
to make me keep sowing on,
I've drank the cup of disappointment and pain
and gone many a day without a song,
But I've sipped enough nectar from the roses of
life that makes me want to keep living on. -*
Author Unknown

19 POEM WRITTEN BY MY SISTER

My Sister
Ina Moore Baygents

This is a person I know so well
She's my sister so the story I can tell.
We grew up with a loving mother and dad the
very best life any kids could have had.
We never dreamed we'd part some day,
But we married and went out own way.
I'd look so forward to the visit we had,
When she'd go home I missed her badly.
We never know what God has in mind,
But we do know His way is the best we can find.
She was widowed at a very young age,

The heart aches she had would take a whole page.
God blessed her with four little girls and one little boy,
Though life was hard they gave her joy.
She worked hard to keep them clothes to wear,
but they were washed and ironed with loving care.
A roof over their head and shoes on their feet she worked every day from sun up to sunset.
It seemed her work was never done.
She never let them feel that life for them was bad instead she taught them to thank God for all that they had.
Many nights she stayed on her knees praying to God to supply their needs,
God was so good and heard her call,
He made sure she would never fall.
She taught her children to have faith in the Lord and to Him in the end there's a great reward.
When the church doors open they were there with pretty clothes and the girls bows in their hair,
Deb's daddy died before she came into the world and he never had the chance to see this little girl.
When she talked about him it made her sad just to think she never knew her dad.

She had an old papa that filled in the gap many days she sat in his lap.
He told her stories of days gone by and when she thinks of Mama and Papa it makes her cry.
They have gone on now to be with the Lord and in heaven they're reaping a just reward.
Someday we will meet them; how happy we will be those precious ole faces once more to see.
Maude's hard work has brought her earth's reward she is truly loved by her four girls and a boy.
Her grandchildren think she's the best Granny kids ever had and if you mess with Granny it will sure make them mad.
I love my sister as you can plainly tell,
My thoughts and love go with her and I do wish her well.
So may this birthday be one she'll cherish in her heart because it was planned by her children who know they'll never part.
When they all get to heaven she'll greet them with open arms,
Saying, 'Come in children I'm waiting for you with your father.'
She never had welfare and her kids never ate free at school,

And she taught them to live by the golden rule.
To always be honest and your daily bread earn,
That's a good lesson in life for all to learn.
It's true they grew up without a dad,
But they had the best mother kids ever had,
Now they are all five children and work for what they eat,
The lesson Mama taught them you could never beat.
I close this with eyes full of tears,
Saying, 'I love all,' Aunt Ina.

Written by your sister,
Ina Mae Moore Baygents
For your 75th birthday
April 18, 2002

20 GEMS FROM PAULETTE

Paulette found this first poem for me and wrote the next as a gift and I love them more than any gift she could have bought.

Mother's Bible Is a Gem
Author Unknown
There is a treasure oh so sweet the heart is does amaze that's lying in mother's bedroom her Bible worn with age,
She'd quietly steal away each day about the set of sun to read the book she treasured most; she knew that her race would one day be run.
The pages turned with feeble hands as she searched it through and through;

And studied over and over again till ever Psalm she knew.
One day an angel will come to call my mother home to share in all the beauties of that land that Jesus has prepared,
She will leave us lonely, weeping and sad and we'll miss her everyday but we know she'll walk that street of gold; her Bible led the way.
Daddy wasn't there for her and he waits in heaven for mother at the gate inside,
With boundless love and care and as he stands there oh, so patiently with his arms held open wide.
The finger prints she'll leave behind the tears that stained the page, mother's Bible is a gem and I'll treasure it always.

To Father on Her Special Day
By Paulette Massey Anderson

I'm writing you a poem to say have a Happy father's day,
There are things our dad should do but instead you filled his shoes.

JESUS AND ME

And did so well in his position when he left we missed him so,
No one could have guessed a pretty girl could be the best,
At doing stuff reserved for Dad without driving us mad.
And we're not sure who spread the lie about how dad should be a guy,
Because even though you wear a bra we couldn't ask for a better pa.
The calendar might clearly say this is father's day,
And you might think it weird,
That you will get two special days to honor you this year.
A lifetime wouldn't be enough to show how much you mean to us,
We don't care if you're a girl
You are still the best dad in the whole world!
I love you very much and always will.

Paulette Massey Anderson

PAULETTE MASSEY ANDERSON

Maude Moore Massey in 1957

21 POEM THE WIDOW

The Widow
By: R.D. Jones 1966

Have you ever known a widow, who was a woman indeed who has suffered many a heartache, which has lived with many a need? Who has raised all her children in the ways of God, not man, well I know of such a woman, whom by the grace of God can.
Many years ago God visited her,
you see,
And tugged at her young heart and asked,
'Will a child to me you be?'

She knelt at that old altar and freely the tears did flow and gave her life to Jesus, yes that's been many a year ago,
The tears that rolled down her cheeks was not tears of sorrow you see but tears of joy and happiness, when Jesus told her, 'I love thee.'
Jesus has always loved, protected her and guided her along the way yes, He is still with her now and will never go away.
One day God called her husband and took him to heaven above, yet Jesus stayed with this woman, who cried out to him with love.
Yes He stayed with her in her hours of despair, when she cried, 'Jesus, I love you,' she could feel Him there.
I know this Christian sister has had many trials along the way but Jesus has a crown of righteousness laid up for her one day.
If she will be true and faithful and never go astray she will be able to live with Jesus and meet her loved ones up there one day.
Yes, she has raised all of her children,
To be good God fearing women and men to believe that Jesus our Savior loves them, as no mortal human can.

JESUS AND ME

Soon they will all be married and gone and find themselves a home,
But this sister will still love Jesus;
He will never leave her alone.
Yes Sister Maude Massey, may God bless you and keep facing this world with a song and a smile. Always remember Jesus loves and will never leave you,
No, not even in your greatest trial.

ABOUT THE AUTHOR

Maude Massey stayed in the home she and her beloved Delbert built, as she promised him, until their children were raised. Upon her retirement, Maude sold the old home stead. When the new owners removed the floor covering, the scuff marks made by the toes of Delbert's work boots, as he knelt in prayer, were still visible. Every day before going to work, Delbert prayed and concluded every prayer, "Lord, hedge my children in from the ways of the world." When the last child married and left home, Maude's children moved her to be near them, where she is lovingly cared for by all. Maude Massey is matriarch to five generations and, as biblically promised, 'Her children call her blessed.'

JESUS AND ME

MAUDE MASSEY

To order, contact:
Sue Massey Crocker
P.O. Box 372
Gautier, Ms. 39553
Phone: 228-497-4369
maudemassey@yahoo.com

Made in the USA
Columbia, SC
17 July 2025